Editor
Eric Migliaccio

Managing Editor
Ina Massler Levin, M.A.

Editor-in-Chief
Sharon Coan, M.S. Ed.

Cover Artist
Janet Chadwick

Art Manager
Kevin Barnes

Art Director
CJae Froshay

Imaging
Rosa C. See

Product Manager
Phil Garcia

Publishers
Rachelle Cracchiolo, M.S. Ed.
Mary Dupuy Smith, M.S. Ed.

GRADE 6

Author

Debra J. Housel, M.S. Ed.

Teacher Created Materials, Inc.
6421 Industry Way
Westminster, CA 92683
www.teachercreated.com
ISBN-0-7439-3776-0
©2003 Teacher Created Materials, Inc.
Made in U.S.A.

The classroom teacher may reproduce copies of materials in this book for classroom use only. The reproduction of any part for an entire school or school system is strictly prohibited. No part of this publication may be transmitted, stored, or recorded in any form without written permission from the publisher.

Teacher Created Materials

Table of Contents

Introduction

The old adage "practice makes perfect" can really hold true for your child's education. The more practice and exposure your child has with concepts being taught in school, the more success he or she is likely to find. As a parent, it is difficult to know where to focus your efforts so that the extra practice your child receives at home supports what he or she is learning in school.

This book has been written to help parents and teachers reinforce basic skills with children. *Practice Makes Perfect: Spelling* covers basic spelling skills for sixth graders. The exercises in this book can be completed in any order. The practice included in this book will meet or reinforce educational standards and objectives similar to the ones required by your state and school district for sixth graders:

- The student will know how to spell many of the most frequently misspelled words in English.

- The student will recognize the spelling patterns for common word beginnings and endings.

- The student will accurately spell multi-syllabic words.

- The student will spell high-frequency words, the 3,000 words that make up more than 90 percent of all written material. High-frequency words make up the majority of the spelling words in each lesson.

Since educational research has shown that memorizing syllables is the best way to learn to spell multi-syllabic words, every lesson includes the syllabication of the words based on *The American Heritage Dictionary*.

How to Make the Most of This Book

Here are some ideas for making the most of this book:

- Set aside a specific place in your home to work on this book. Keep it neat and tidy, with the necessary materials on hand.

- Determine a specific time of day to work on these practice pages to establish consistency. Look for times in your day or week that are less hectic and more conducive to practicing skills.

- Keep all practice sessions with your child positive and constructive. If your child becomes frustrated or tense, do not force your child to perform. Set the book aside and try again another time.

- Review and praise the work your child has done.

- Allow the child to use whatever writing instrument he or she prefers. For example, writing with gel pens on black paper adds variety and pleasure to drill work.

- Introduce the spelling words in the list. Discuss how the words are different and how they are alike. Read the "In Context" column together. Be sure that the students understand the meaning of each word.

- Have the child memorize each word in chunks. Study the syllables shown in each lesson and practice putting the pieces together.

- If necessary, help the child to read and comprehend the directions and exercises.

- Encourage the child to point out spelling words, past and present, in the books, newspapers, and magazines he or she reads.

Spelling Demons

The following are some of the most commonly misspelled English words.

Word	Syllables	In Context
foreign	for•eign	Do you know how to speak any **foreign** languages?
weird	weird	He had on a very **weird** outfit.
separate	sep•a•rate	Put their gifts in two **separate** bags.
calendar	cal•en•dar	The **calendar** pictured a different dog each month.
a lot	a lot	It took **a lot** of hours to paint the house.
embarrass	em•bar•rass	It will **embarrass** me if I have to get up on stage.
guarantee	guar•an•tee	Did this toaster come with a money-back **guarantee**?
privilege	priv•i•lege	She had the **privilege** of driving her dad's car to school.
rhythm	rhy•thm	The drum player had a natural sense of **rhythm**.
license	li•cense	When you are 16 you can apply for a driver's **license**.
vacuum	vac•u•um	Please **vacuum** the living room.
irrelevant	ir•rel•e•vant	Get rid of **irrelevant** information in your essay.
accommodate	ac•com•mo•date	The room can **accommodate** four people.
familiar	fa•mil•iar	Something about that woman is **familiar** to me.
appropriate	ap•pro•pri•ate	Wearing jeans isn't **appropriate** for attending a funeral.

Write the spelling word that begins and ends with same letters as the word given. Some of the spelling words begin and end with the same letters. In that case, an additional line was given.

Example: little _____license_____ (*license* is used again below)

1. four   _____

2. airplane _____

             _____

3. vandalism _____

4. late   _____

5. shuttle   _____

6. Internet _____

7. gauge   _____

8. chair   _____

9. flatten   _____

10. express _____

11. petite   _____

12. wild   _____

13. rum   _____

14. What spelling word in this lesson is actually two small words? _____

Spelling Demons *(cont.)*

Roman Numeral Code

Change the Roman numeral code into spelling words from this lesson. Write each letter beneath the Roman numeral that stands for it.

I = a	II = b	III = c	IV = d	V = e	VI = f	VII = g	VIII = h	IX = i
X = j	XI = k	XII = l	XIII = m	XIV = n	XV = o	XVI = p	XVII = q	XVIII = r
XIX = s	XX = t	XXI = u	XXII = v	XXIII = w	XXIV = x	XXV = y	XXVI = z	

Example: XIX   XV   XII   IV   IX   V   XVIII
          s   o   l   d   i   e   r

1. XII IX III V XIV XIX V

2. VII XXI I XVIII I XIV XX V V

3. I XVI XVI XVIII XV XVI XVIII IX I XX V

4. III I XII V XIV IV I XVIII

5. XXII I III XXI XXI XIII

6. XXIII V IX XVIII IV

7. IX XVIII XVIII V XII V XXII I XIV XX

8. XVIII VIII XXV XX VIII XIII

9. V XIII II I XVIII XVIII I XIX XIX

10. I   XII XV XX

11. I III III XV XIII XIII XV IV I XX V

12. XVI XVIII IX XXII IX XII V VII V

13. VI I XIII IX XII IX I XVIII

14. VI XV XVIII V IX VII XIV

15. XIX V XVI I XVIII I XX V

Word Beginning: "un"

Often the word beginning "un" means "not."

Word	Syllables	In Context
unusual	un•u•su•al	It was **unusual** for their dog to bark so much.
untied	un•tied	The person **untied** the horse from its post.
unknown	un•known	Where he went next is **unknown**.
unhappy	un•hap•py	You look **unhappy**. Is something wrong?
unable	un•a•ble	She was **unable** to climb that high.
unexpected	un•ex•pect•ed	The package was **unexpected**.
unreliable	un•re•li•a•ble	Her car is so **unreliable** that it's always in the shop.
uncertain	un•cer•tain	Jane is **uncertain** when she'll return from Europe.
uncommon	un•com•mon	It's **uncommon** for a newborn to weigh 11 pounds.
unkempt	un•kempt	We could barely move through the **unkempt** room.
unfortunately	un•for•tu•nate•ly	I had, **unfortunately**, lost my keys the day before.
unreasonable	un•rea•son•a•ble	It's **unreasonable** to expect her to walk 16 miles.
uninjured	un•in•jured	Fortunately the baby was **uninjured** by the fall.
unwelcome	un•wel•come	Don't frown, or you'll make her feel **unwelcome**.
unmistakable	un•mis•tak•able	Since his outfit is **unmistakable**, I know I saw him.

Two words are **synonyms** if they have similar meanings. Two words are **antonyms** if they have opposite meanings. Adding "un" to many words creates their antonyms. Add "un" to the following words to form antonyms and spelling words from this lesson.

Word		Antonym
1. certain	+ "un" =	
2. reliable	+ "un" =	
3. expected	+ "un" =	
4. welcome	+ "un" =	
5. usual	+ "un" =	
6. able	+ "un" =	
7. common	+ "un" =	
8. tied	+ "un" =	
9. reasonable	+ "un" =	
10. fortunately	+ "un" =	
11. mistakable	+ "un" =	
12. happy	+ "un" =	
13. injured	+ "un" =	
14. known	+ "un" =	

15. What spelling word is missing from the list above? _____

16. What is its antonym? _____

Word Beginning: "un" (cont.)

Word Scramble

Unscramble the words to form spelling words from this lesson. Put the numbered letters on the lines below to find the answer to the riddle.

Example: odunne   <u>u</u>   <u>n</u>   <u>d</u>   <u>o</u>   <u>n</u>   <u>e</u>

1. inuerundj   __ __ __ __ __ __ __ __ __
        1

2. wecomulne   __ __ __ __ __ __ __ __ __
     2

3. kunptem   __ __ __ __ __ __ __
       3

4. tamesnublaki   __ __ __ __ __ __ __ __ __ __ __ __
            4

5. labenu   __ __ __ __ __ __

6. sunluua   __ __ __ __ __ __ __

7. encurtain   __ __ __ __ __ __ __ __ __
     5

8. realunbail   __ __ __ __ __ __ __ __ __ __
       6

9. united*   __ __ __ __ __ __
    7

10. unceptdeex   __ __ __ __ __ __ __ __ __ __
         8

11. pyhunap   __ __ __ __ __ __ __
    9

12. mounnmoc   __ __ __ __ __ __ __ __

13. ulatenufortyn   __ __ __ __ __ __ __ __ __ __ __ __ __
             10

14. nowunnk   __ __ __ __ __ __ __
      11

15. osearbunlane   __ __ __ __ __ __ __ __ __ __ __ __

*This is already a word, but rearrange the letters to make it into a spelling word from this lesson.

Riddle: What was the weather forecast for Mexico?

__ __ __ __ __   __ __ __ __ __ __ ,
5   9   6   2   6   7   11   8   4   10

__ __ __   __ __ __ __ __ __
9   11   7   7   4   3   4   2   1

Word Beginning: "dis"

Word	Syllables	In Context
discuss	dis•cuss	Let's **discuss** our plans for the holidays.
disaster	dis•as•ter	A strong hurricane is a natural **disaster**.
discovery	dis•cov•er•y	The **discovery** of North America changed the world.
disrupt	dis•rupt	Please don't **disrupt** the speaker.
disturb	dis•turb	Don't **disturb** your mom; she's still asleep.
disease	dis•ease	Smallpox is a deadly **disease**.
distinct	dis•tinct	I could see two **distinct** outlines in the shadows.
dissolve	dis•solve	Salt will **dissolve** in water.
distribute	dis•trib•ute	The charity will **distribute** food and clothes to the needy.
discouraged	dis•cour•aged	Earning a 75 means you passed, so don't be **discouraged**.
disappointed	dis•ap•point•ed	When she didn't get a kitten, she felt **disappointed**.

Sometimes the word beginning "dis" means "not."

Word	Syllables	In Context
disadvantage	dis•ad•van•tage	If you start early, it puts the other racers at a **disadvantage**.
disapproved	dis•ap•proved	Their dad **disapproved** of the twin's late bedtime.
dissatisfied	dis•sat•is•fied	The customer was **dissatisfied** with the product.
disorganized	dis•or•gan•ized	She can't find anything because she's so **disorganized**.

Circle the word that's spelled correctly. Copy it on the line.

1. disaproved   disapproved   disaprovd   _____ _____
2. disadvantage   disadvantedge   disadvantege   _____
3. disolve   dissulve   dissolve   _____
4. distinkt   distinct   distint   _____
5. dicuss   discus   discuss   _____
6. diseaze   dissease   disease   _____
7. dissatisfied   disatisfied   disatsfied   _____
8. distribute   distribut   distribuit   _____
9. discuraged   discouraged   discoureged   _____
10. disapointed   disappointed   disappointed   _____
11. disrut   disrupt   disrumpt   _____
12. discovry   discovery   discuvery   _____
13. disturb   distrub   disturbt   _____
14. disorgenized   disorganized   disorganised   _____
15. dissaster   disasster   disaster   _____

Word Beginning: **"dis"** *(cont.)*

Different Kinds of Sentences

Write spelling words 1–5 in **exclamatory** sentences. An exclamatory sentence communicates strong emotion or surprise. **Example:** *We've got to get out of the store right away!*

Exclamatory Sentences End with an Exclamation Point

1. _____
2. _____
3. _____
4. _____
5. _____

Write spelling words 6–10 in **declarative** sentences. A declarative sentence makes a statement. **Example:** *We went to the store.*

Declarative Sentences End with a Period

6. _____
7. _____
8. _____
9. _____
10. _____

Write spelling words 11–15 in **interrogative** sentences. An interrogative sentence asks a question. **Example:** *Did you go to the store?*

Interrogative Sentences End with a Question Mark

11. _____
12. _____
13. _____
14. _____
15. _____

Word Beginning: "mis"

Often the word beginning "mis" means "wrong."

Word	Syllables	In Context
misplaced	mis•placed	My grandmother **misplaced** her glasses again.
misbehaves	mis•be•haves	My little brother often **misbehaves** in church.
misspelled	mis•spelled	The brochure had two **misspelled** words.
misjudged	mis•judged	Suddenly Tina knew she'd **misjudged** the man.
misleading	mis•lead•ing	That ad is so **misleading**!
misinterpret	mis•in•ter•pret	Please don't **misinterpret** what I'm about to say.
misunderstanding	mis•un•der•stand•ing	They had a serious **misunderstanding**.
mistakes	mis•takes	Jake made two **mistakes** on his test paper.
misery	mis•er•y	I never knew **misery** until I got the flu.
miserable	mis•er•a•ble	Chickenpox makes you feel **miserable** and itchy.
mischievous	mis•chie•vous	His little sister is **mischievous**.
miscellaneous	mis•cell•a•ne•ous	Put these papers in the folder marked **miscellaneous**.
misgivings	mis•giv•ings	I had **misgivings** about a cat and a rabbit living together.
Mississippi	Mis•sis•sip•pi	The **Mississippi** River is North America's longest river.
Missouri	Mis•sou•ri	**Missouri** is a Midwestern state in the U.S.A.

Copy the spelling words in order in the first column. Look at the word in the second column. Decide if each pair of words are **synonyms** (similar in meaning) or **antonyms** (opposite in meaning). Put a check mark (✓) in one of the last two columns to indicate your choice. You may use a thesaurus or dictionary to look up the meaning of the spelling word.

Spelling Word	Word	Synonym	Antonym
Example mismatched	clash	✔	
1.	found		
2.	behaves		
3.	misprint, error		
4.	miscalculate		
5.	deceptive		
6.	misconstrue		
7.	understanding		
8.	corrections		
9.	joy		
10.	happy		
11.	naughty		
12.	various, assorted		
13.	worry, apprehension		

14. Write the names of the states: _____ & _____

Word Beginning: "mis" *(cont.)*

Syllable Cymbals

Write each spelling word on the cymbal that matches its number of syllables. Write the syllables within each word using different colors. On the drum below, write the two words that have five syllables.

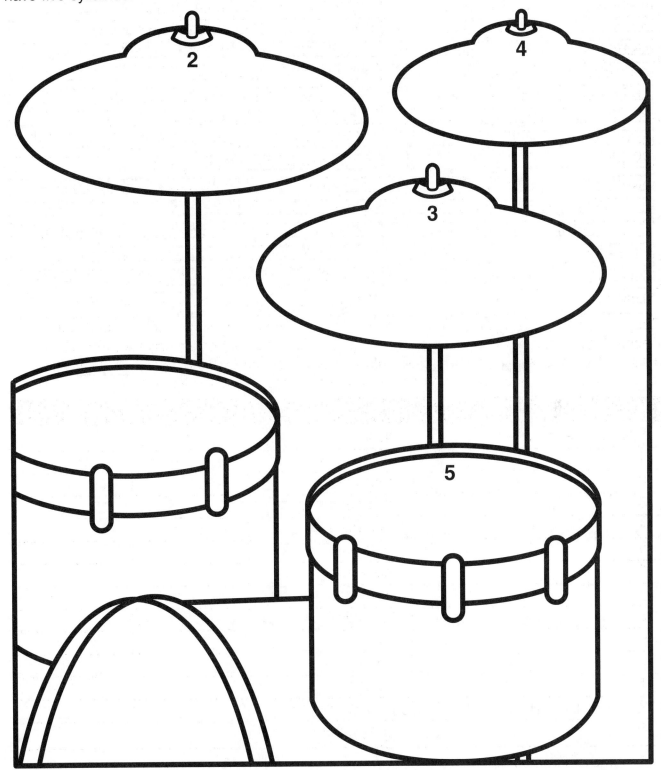

Word Beginning: "com"

Word	Syllables	In Context
complete	com•plete	After I finish this page, my project will be **complete**.
compare	com•pare	Let's **compare** our results to see if they differ.
compass	com•pass	She used the **compass** to find her way out of the woods.
companion	com•pan•ion	Did you notice who his **companion** was?
company	com•pan•y	He started an Internet **company** last spring.
combined	com•bined	Vinegar **combined** with baking soda causes a reaction.
complex	com•plex	Do you know how to do this **complex** math equation?
command	com•mand	The officer was in **command** of 54 soldiers.
committee	com•mit•tee	The **committee** met to decide how to spend the funds.
computer	com•pu•ter	Did you get a new **computer**?
comparison	com•par•i•son	You can get the best price by **comparison** shopping.
comments	com•ments	The woman refused to give any **comments** to the press.
complicated	com•pli•cat•ed	The situation in the Middle East is quite **complicated**.
communicate	com•mu•ni•cate	You must **communicate** what you want to do.
communication	com•mu•ni•ca•tion	Instant messaging is a popular type of **communication**.

All of these spelling words begin the same. Some share the same ending letter. Write the spelling words on the appropriate lines.

1. Write the spelling word that ends in "y": _____

2. Write the spelling word that ends in "x": _____

3. Write the spelling word that ends in "r": _____

4. Write the 2 spelling words that end in "s": _____ & _____

5. Write the 3 spelling words that end in "n": _____,

_____, & _____

6. Write the 3 spelling words that end in "d": _____,

_____, & _____

7. Write the 4 spelling words that end in "e": _____, _____,

_____, & _____

Word Beginning: "com" (cont.)

Crossword Puzzle

Across

2. The president of the United States is in _____ of all of the armed forces.
4. Another name for pets is _____ animals.
6. Do you live in the large apartment _____ on Union Street?
7. The restaurant manager would like to hear your _____ about your meal.
8. The doctors decided to do a _____ operation to save the boy's life.
10. Satellites have greatly sped up long-distance _____ .
12. Last year the _____ gave its workers bonus checks at the end of the year.
13. She's the chairperson of the school improvement _____ .

Down

1. The heat _____ with the high humidity made the day very uncomfortable.
2. The _____ showed that they were heading northeast.
3. If you _____ these two tops, you'll see that one is definitely larger.
5. How will we _____ with each other while you're gone?
6. Did you shut the _____ down after you finished using the Internet?
9. In _____ to tart red cherries, dark cherries are sweeter.
11. I need some bowls to _____ my china set.

Word Beginnings: "inter" & "self"

The word beginning "inter" means "between" in some words (Examples: international, interview, intersection). The word beginning "self" is almost always followed by a hyphen and another word. (Exception: selfish)

Word	Syllables	In Context
interesting	in•ter•est•ing	Which of the books did you find the most **interesting**?
international	in•ter•na•tion•al	They delayed the **international** flight to Peru.
intersection	in•ter•sec•tion	That **intersection** really needs a traffic light.
interrupt	in•ter•rupt	Please do not **interrupt** me while I'm speaking.
internal	in•ter•nal	The jet ski looks fine, so the damage must be **internal.**
interpreter	in•ter•pret•er	We'll need a sign language **interpreter** for our deaf client.
intervene	in•ter•vene	If I don't **intervene**, the dog may bite the child.
interview	in•ter•view	My brother has a job **interview** at 10 A.M.
interior	in•te•ri•or	This used car's **interior** looks brand new!
Internet	In•ter•net	The worldwide web is also called the **Internet**.
self-employed	self-em•ployed	Martha is **self-employed**; she recently opened a bakery.
self-defense	self-de•fense	She shot the man in **self-defense**.
self-control	self-con•trol	It takes **self-control** to stick to a diet.
self-confidence	self-con•fi•dence	It's good to have **self-confidence** in your abilities.
self-sufficient	self-suf•fi•cient	He wants to be **self-sufficient** by growing his own food.

Is the **boldfaced** word spelled wrong? If it is not correct, write it correctly in the middle column. If it is right, circle **OK**.

1. Do you think you did well at the **intervew**?		OK
2. You spend a lot of hours surfing the **Internet**.		OK
3. A deaf woman needs an **interpreter** for the ceremony.		OK
4. It takes **self-confidense** to perform on the stage.		OK
5. What an **intersting** idea!		OK
6. He fought back in **self-defence**.		OK
7. We will ship to **international** buyers.		OK
8. My mother is **self-employed**; she owns a bookstore.		OK
9. There've been too many crashes at that **intrsection**.		OK
10. The house's **intereor** was surprisingly shabby.		OK
11. The doctor lost her **self-control** and yelled at the man.		OK
12. Please do not **interupt** another person's speech.		OK
13. The doctor's name was listed under **internal** medicine.		OK
14. As a child grows, he becomes more **self-sufficent**.		OK
15. Please **interveen** and stop their fight!		OK

Word Beginnings: "inter" & "self" *(cont.)*

Word Scale

Count the number of spelling words that begin with "inter." Count the number of spelling words that begin with "self." Which group has more? Fill in the balance, grouping the words by their beginnings. Be sure to put the group with the most words on the heavier side.

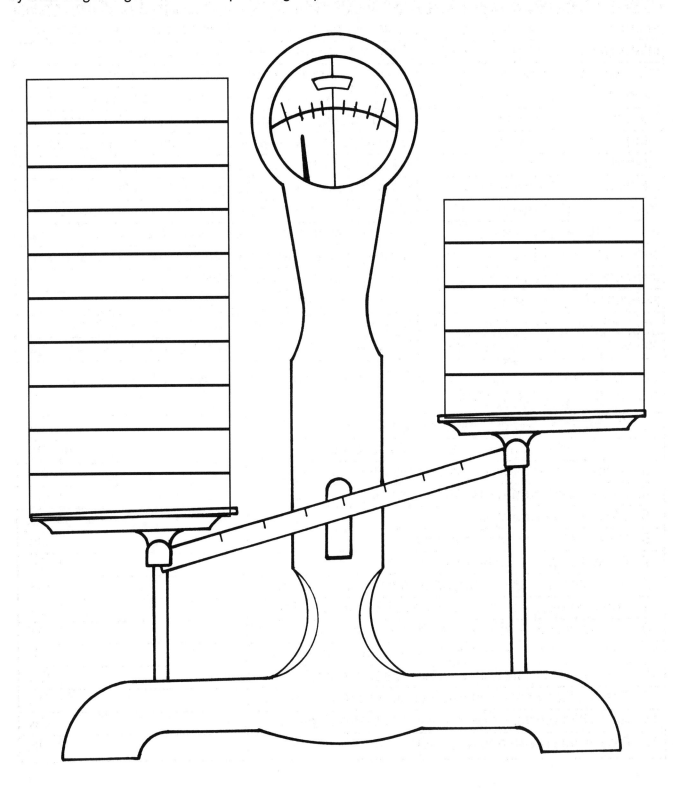

Word Ending: "age"

The word ending "age" is pronounced "edge."

Word	Syllables	In Context
language	lan•guage	Can you read and write the Chinese **language**?
average	av•er•age	Her grades in science improved until they were **average**.
message	mes•sage	Didn't you get the phone **message** I left for you?
package	pack•age	It costs a lot to ship a **package** from here to Asia.
manager	man•ag•er	After we hired Ken as our **manager**, our profits rose.
courage	cour•age	Firefighters show **courage** when they enter burning buildings.
encourage	en•cour•age	My teachers always **encourage** me to read more often.
mortgage	mort•gage	The **mortgage** on this house will be paid off in 25 years.
damage	dam•age	Fortunately the storm caused little **damage**.
voyage	voy•age	Since this is my first cruise, I expect this **voyage** to be exciting.
marriage	mar•riage	The **marriage** took place on July 16,1993.
advantage	ad•van•tage	Is there any **advantage** to using this one instead of that one?
carriage	car•riage	Suddenly the horse-drawn **carriage** hit a rut and broke a wheel.
luggage	lug•gage	The airline said that we had too many pieces of **luggage**.
beverage	bev•er•age	Ice cold milk is my favorite **beverage**.

Choose the best word from the list above to complete each sentence. Write it on the line. Use each word once. Skip those you can't figure out and go back to them once you've done the others.

1. Hot cocoa is a popular _____ during the wintertime.

2. I tried to _____ Phil to try out for the school musical.

3. My parents went on an around-the-world _____.

4. The airline lost my _____! Now what'll I do for clothing?

5. My grandparents' _____ lasted for 60 years.

6. What _____ do you speak?

7. I've brought my social studies grade point _____ up to 83.

8. The post office refused to take the large, heavy_____.

9. Fortunately, the _____ caused by the crash was minor.

10. The _____ bumped and swayed over the trail's many ruts.

11. He's not at home. May I take a _____ for him?

12. The soldiers showed _____ during the fierce battle.

13. Act now to take _____ of these incredible savings!

14. My dad is the _____ of that restaurant.

Word Ending: "age" (cont.)

Word Scramble

Unscramble the words below to form spelling words from this lesson. Put the numbered letters on the lines below to find the answer to the riddle.

Example: etrax   c   a   b   b   a   g   e

1. gormetag   __ __ __ __(1) __ __ __

2. rageairc   __ __(2) __ __ __ __ __

3. gagegul   __ __ __ __ __ __ __

4. massege   __ __ __ __(3) __ __ __

5. gearuco   __ __ __(4) __ __ __

6. maregiar   __ __ __ __ __(5) __ __

7. erabgeev   __(6) __ __ __ __ __ __

8. lagenuag   __ __(7) __ __ __ __ __

9. gaevyo   __ __ __ __ __(8) __

10. gramnea   __ __ __(9) __ __ __

11. gamade   __ __ __ __ __

12. erangecou   __ __ __ __(10) __ __ __ __ __

13. tanavgead   __ __ __ __ __ __ __ __ __

14. cagekpa   __ __ __ __ __ __ __

15. agerave   __ __ __ __(11) __ __ __

Riddle: Where did the lobster get a ride?

__ __ __   __ __ __ __ __ __ __ __ __
(7)(1)(7)   (2)(11)(4)(3)(1)(7)(2)(8)(7)(9)

__ __ __   __ __ __ __ __ __ __
(6)(4)(3)   (3)(1)(7)(1)(5)(10)(9)

Word Ending: "ary"

Word	Syllables	n Context
vary	var•y	The color doesn't **vary** much from one printing to the next.
dictionary	dic•tion•ar•y	I'll look that word up in my **dictionary**.
necessary	nec•es•sar•y	For this particular sickness, medicine is **necessary**.
library	li•brar•y	She just borrowed 65 books from the **library**!
ordinary	or•din•ar•y	It looked like an **ordinary** piece of paper.
extraordinary	ex•traor•din•ar•y	Nothing **extraordinary** happened today.
military	mil•i•tar•y	She joined the **military** about six months ago.
vocabulary	vo•cab•u•lar•y	The more you read, the more your **vocabulary** will grow.
primary	pri•mar•y	The **primary** reason to move is that we need more space.
elementary	el•e•men•tar•y	Morgan attends a nearby **elementary** school.
temporary	tem•po•rar•y	Luckily, this tiny office is just **temporary**.
imaginary	i•mag•i•nar•y	Jonah, who is three years old, has two **imaginary** friends.
stationary	sta•tion•ar•y	Since it is **stationary**, that gate is for decoration only.
solitary	sol•i•tar•y	Hamsters are **solitary** animals that like living alone.
contemporary	con•tem•po•rar•y	Do you prefer a **contemporary** (*modern*) home?

Copy the spelling words in the order they appear above. Number them in order from A–Z. You may need to look as far as the third letter. Then write the words in A–Z order.

Word	Number	A–Z Order
1.		
2.		
3.		
4.		
5.		
6.		
7.		
8.		
9.		
10.		
11.		
12.		
13.		
14.		
15.		

Word Ending: "ary" (cont.)

Roman Numeral Code

Change the Roman numeral code into spelling words from this lesson. Write each letter beneath the Roman numeral that stands for it.

I = a	II = b	III = c	IV = d	V = e	VI = f	VII = g	VIII = h	IX = i
X = j	XI = k	XII = l	XIII = m	XIV = n	XV = o	XVI = p	XVII = q	XVIII = r
XIX = s	XX = t	XXI = u	XXII = v	XXIII = w	XXIV = x	XXV = y	XXVI = z	

Example: III I XIV I XVIII XXV

    c a n a r y

1. XV XVIII IV IX XIV I XVIII XXV

9. XXII I XVIII XXV

2. V XII V XIII V XIV XX I XVIII XXV

10. IX XIII I VII IX XIV I XVIII XXV

3. IV IX III XX IX XV XIV I XVIII XXV

11. XXII XV III I II XXI XII I XVIII XXV

4. III XV XIV XX V XIII XVI XV XVIII I XVIII XXV

12. XIX XX I XX IX XV XIV I XVIII XXV

5. XII IX II XVIII I XVIII XXV

13. XX V XIII XVI XV XVIII I XVIII XXV

6. XVI XVIII IX XIII I XVIII XXV

14. XIV V III V XIX XIX I XVIII XXV

7. XIX XV XII IX XX I XVIII XXV

15. XIII IX XII IX XX I XVIII XXV

8. V XXIV XX XVIII I XV XVIII IV IX XIV I XVIII XXV

Word Endings: "ion" & "ize"

The word ending "ion" is usually pronounced "yun." The word ending "ize" is pronounced "eyes."

Word	Syllables	In Context
onions	on•ions	The cook added **onions** to the recipe.
billion	bil•lion	Today there are over six **billion** people living on Earth.
millionaire	mil•lion•aire	By winning the contest, she became a **millionaire**.
champion	cham•pi•on	Jack's dog is a show **champion**.
pavilion	pa•vil•ion	We reserved a picnic **pavilion** for June 28.
fashion	fa•shion	Do you like that new **fashion**?
opinion	o•pin•ion	In my **opinion**, we should start over again.
region	re•gion	I cannot find that brand in this **region** of the state.
religion	re•lig•ion	People sometimes disagree about **religion**.
memorize	mem•o•rize	I'll help you to **memorize** these spelling words.
realize	re•al•ize	Bailey didn't **realize** that his questions were rude.
recognize	rec•og•nize	At first, Jamie didn't **recognize** the picture.
apologize	a•pol•o•gize	Sam will **apologize** to Carly.
organize	or•gan•ize	Let's **organize** this room to get rid of all this clutter.
emphasize	em•pha•size	Using bold print helps to **emphasize** text.

Circle the word that's spelled correctly. Copy it on the line.

1. opnion   opinon   opinion   _____

2. fashun   fashion   fashin   _____

3. regon   rejion   region   _____

4. religion   religon   religin   _____

5. aplogize   apologize   apologise   _____

6. emphasize   emphasise   emphazize   _____

7. billion   bilion   billiun   _____

8. reconize   recognize   recognise   _____

9. onuns   oniuns   onions   _____

10. organise   organize   orgenize   _____

11. chamion   champeon   champion   _____

12. pavilion   pavillion   pavlion   _____

13. realise   realize   relize   _____

14. millionare   millionaire   milionaire   _____

15. memorize   memorise   memrize   _____

Word Endings: "ion" & "ize" *(cont.)*

Crossword Puzzle

Across

2. Do you _____ how important this is?
3. The number one _____ has nine zeroes.
4. If you bump into someone else, you really should _____ .
6. Peeling _____ may cause you to shed some tears.
8. The tennis _____ received a gold cup.
11. A _____ is anyone who has a million (or more) dollars.
13. I plan to attend the _____ show at noon.

Down

1. The desert is the driest _____ in that nation.
2. The priest devoted his life to his _____ .
5. The children were so mud-covered that their parents couldn't _____ them.
7. Shane began to _____ his papers in folders.
9. We bought corn dogs at the fair's food _____ .
10. In my _____ , black fingernail polish looks weird.
11. For extra credit, the student was asked to _____ 100 lines of poetry.
12. I want to _____ that spelling will count in your project's grade.

Word Ending: "ous"

The word ending "ous" is pronounced "us" and means "full of."

Word	Syllables	In Context
famous	fa•mous	A **famous** actress is signing photographs over there.
nervous	ner•vous	I felt **nervous** about staying alone in the haunted house.
enormous	e•nor•mous	Finding the lost son was an **enormous** relief to the parents.
numerous	nu•mer•ous	It took **numerous** attempts to finish hanging the wallpaper.
fabulous	fab•u•lous	You look **fabulous** wearing that shade of blue.
jealous	jeal•ous	Lydia was **jealous** of all the attention the baby was getting.
dangerous	dan•ger•ous	It's **dangerous** to walk on the road at night wearing dark clothes.
ridiculous	ri•dic•u•lous	He looked **ridiculous** wearing the clown suit.
hideous	hid•e•ous	I think those drapes are **hideous**!
gorgeous	gor•geous	On the other hand, those curtains are **gorgeous**.
courageous	cou•ra•geous	It took a **courageous** effort to keep them both afloat.
courteous	cour•te•ous	The boys were **courteous** to the people in the nursing home.
continuous	con•tin•u•ous	The refrigerator's humming noise was **continuous**.
outrageous	out•ra•geous	Ben paid an **outrageous** price for his car.
marvelous	mar•vel•ous	We had a **marvelous** time at the amusement park.

Write the spelling word that begins and ends with same letters as the word given. Some of the spelling words begin and end with the same letters. In those cases, additional lines are given.

Example: dishes ___dangerous___ (*dangerous* is used again below)

1. gas _____

2. notorious _____

             _____

3. jaws _____

4. radios _____

5. flames _____

             _____

6. octopus _____

7. happiness _____

8. discuss _____

9. moss _____

10. empress _____

11. chorus _____

             _____

Word Ending: "ous" *(cont.)*

Identifying Synonyms and Antonyms

Copy the spelling words in order in the first column. Look at the word in the second column. Decide if each pair of words are **synonyms** (similar in meaning) or **antonyms** (opposite in meaning). Put a check mark (✓) in one of the last two columns to indicate your choice. You may use a thesaurus or dictionary to look up the meaning of the spelling word.

Spelling Word	Word	Synonym	Antonym
Example: tremendous	immense	✓	
1.	unknown		
2.	anxious		
3.	gigantic		
4.	few		
5.	wonderful		
6.	envious		
7.	safe		
8.	silly		
9.	beautiful		
10.	ugly		
11.	cowardly		
12.	rude		
13.	infrequently		
14.	shocking		
15.	great		

Word Ending: "able"

The word ending "able" is added to many words. It sounds like "uh-bull." This combination of letters often stands for "able to be."

Word	Syllables	In Context
vegetables	veg•e•ta•bles	Eating **vegetables** is good for your health.
valuable	val•u•a•ble	Any large diamond is quite **valuable**.
available	a•vail•a•ble	The hotel has two rooms **available**.
comfortable	com•fort•a•ble	I like to wear **comfortable** shoes.
suitable	suit•a•ble	Sneakers are not **suitable** to wear to a formal wedding.
capable	ca•pa•ble	Is your CD **capable** of holding more data?
flammable	flam•ma•ble	Never leave **flammable** objects near a heat source.
acceptable	ac•cept•a•ble	Pinching other people is not **acceptable** behavior.
remarkable	re•mark•a•ble	After the accident Sally made a **remarkable** recovery.
believable	be•liev•a•ble	Her explanation of what happened sounds **believable**.
replaceable	re•place•a•ble	Is the broken part **replaceable**?
changeable	change•a•ble	Today's weather has been very **changeable**.
disposable	dis•pos•a•ble	My baby sister wears **disposable** diapers.
vulnerable	vul•ner•a•ble	You're more **vulnerable** to germs if you don't stay clean.
knowledgeable	knowl•edge•a•ble	Gloria is very **knowledgeable** when it comes to golfing.

Is the **boldfaced** word spelled wrong? If it is not correct, write it correctly in the middle column. If it is right, circle **OK**.

1. Their plans are **changable**.		OK
2. Spray paint is usually **flammable**.		OK
3. The sofa was especially **comfortible**.		OK
4. Is your computer **capable** of running this software?		OK
5. Most batteries are **replacable**.		OK
6. His plan leaves the company **vunerable** to a takeover.		OK
7. Jen doesn't have anything **suitable** to wear to the prom.		OK
8. His story is not very **believable**.		OK
9. That particular coin is quite **valueable**.		OK
10. It's **remarkable** that you've raised your grades so much.		OK
11. The buyer found the price **acceptable**.		OK
12. Paper plates and cups are **disposeable**.		OK
13. Do you have an **available** seat on that flight?		OK
14. The woman seemed quite **knowledgable** about iguanas.		OK
15. The **vegtables** finally started to grow.		OK

Word Ending: "able" *(cont.)*

Word Scramble

Unscramble the words below to form spelling words from this lesson. Put the numbered letters on the lines below to find the answer to the riddle.

Example: lyeslabl   <u>s</u> <u>y</u> <u>l</u> <u>l</u> <u>a</u> <u>b</u> <u>l</u> <u>e</u>

1. usebailt   ___ ___ ___ ___ ___ ___ ___ ___

2. cablepeatc   ___ ___ ___ ___ ___ ___ ___ ___ ___

1

3. foalbertmoc   ___ ___ ___ ___ ___ ___ ___ ___ ___ ___

2

4. wedgelabelonk   ___ ___ ___ ___ ___ ___ ___ ___ ___ ___ ___ ___ ___

5. reaceplealeb   ___ ___ ___ ___ ___ ___ ___ ___ ___ ___ ___

3

6. blivealeeb   ___ ___ ___ ___ ___ ___ ___ ___ ___

4

7. gablesteve   ___ ___ ___ ___ ___ ___ ___ ___ ___

8. leanagecbh   ___ ___ ___ ___ ___ ___ ___ ___ ___

5

9. cleapba   ___ ___ ___ ___ ___ ___ ___

6

10. nearbelluv   ___ ___ ___ ___ ___ ___ ___ ___ ___

7

11. ulabelav   ___ ___ ___ ___ ___ ___ ___ ___

8

12. sealbodsip   ___ ___ ___ ___ ___ ___ ___ ___ ___ ___

9

13. bleakermar   ___ ___ ___ ___ ___ ___ ___ ___ ___ ___

10

14. aveilbaal   ___ ___ ___ ___ ___ ___ ___ ___ ___

11

15. malfambel   ___ ___ ___ ___ ___ ___ ___ ___ ___

Riddle: How did the pig feel after it was in a car crash?

___ ___ ___ ___   ___ ___ ___ ___ ___   ___ ___ ___ ___ ___
3   4   10   8   9   5   11   10   8   7   1   11   6   2   7

Word Ending: "ible"

The word ending "ible" is added to many words. It sounds like short /i/ plus "bull". This combination of letters often stands for "able to be."

Word	Syllables	In Context
possible	pos•si•ble	Is it **possible** to drive there in less than five hours?
impossible	im•pos•si•ble	It's **impossible** to drive from California to Hawaii.
terrible	ter•ri•ble	The tornado caused **terrible** damage to the house.
responsible	re•spon•si•ble	You are **responsible** for feeding your pet.
irresponsible	ir•re•spon•si•ble	It is **irresponsible** not to do your homework.
flexible	flex•i•ble	Let's be **flexible** about the schedule.
incredible	in•cred•i•ble	The hurricane had **incredible** wind speeds.
plausible	plau•si•ble	Their story makes sense, so it's **plausible**.
visible	vis•i•ble	From where we stood, the stream was barely **visible**.
invisible	in•vis•i•ble	No one knows how to become **invisible**.
divisible	div•is•i•ble	The number 4,572 is **divisible** by 9.
sensible	sen•si•ble	Franco did the **sensible** thing by calling the police.
audible	au•di•ble	The sound was so soft it was barely **audible**.
illegible	il•leg•i•ble	Janet's signature is so sloppy it's **illegible**.
edible	ed•i•ble	Are you sure those are **edible** berries that are safe to eat?

Find the spelling word that is the **antonym** (opposite in meaning) of the word given. Write the spelling word on the line. You may use a dictionary or a thesaurus.

1. responsible _____

2. impossible _____

3. inedible _____

4. legible _____

5. invisible _____

6. inflexible _____

7. possible _____

8. visible _____

9. great _____

10. foolish _____

11. inaudible _____

12. ordinary _____

13. implausible _____

14. indivisible _____

15. irresponsible _____

Word Ending: "ible" *(cont.)*

Different Kinds of Sentences

Write spelling words 1–5 in **exclamatory** sentences. An exclamatory sentence communicates strong emotion or surprise. **Example:** *We've got to get out of the store right away!*

Exclamatory Sentences End with an Exclamation Point

1. _____
2. _____
3. _____
4. _____
5. _____

Write spelling words 6–10 in **declarative** sentences. A declarative sentence makes a statement. **Example:** *We went to the store.*

Declarative Sentences End with a Period

6. _____
7. _____
8. _____
9. _____
10. _____

Write spelling words 11–15 in **interrogative** sentences. An interrogative sentence asks a question. **Example:** *Did you go to the store?*

Interrogative Sentences End with a Question Mark

11. _____
12. _____
13. _____
14. _____
15. _____

Word Endings: "sive" & "tual"

Regardless of the "e" at the end, the word ending "sive" is pronounced with a short /i/. The word ending "tual" is pronounced "chew-ull."

Word	Syllables	In Context
inexpensive	in•ex•pen•sive	Why don't you choose the **inexpensive** blouse?
possessive	pos•ses•sive	She's very **possessive** and won't let anyone else touch her stuff.
excessive	ex•ces•sive	Putting on an arm cast for a broken finger is **excessive**.
extensive	ex•ten•sive	The bridge needs **extensive** repairs.
explosives	ex•plo•sives	The **explosives** blew up the old building.
impulsive	im•pul•sive	Josh does things without thinking first. He is so **impulsive**!
massive	mas•sive	It took the **massive** crowd six hours to completely disperse.
offensive	of•fen•sive	Swearing is **offensive** to many people.
persuasive	per•sua•sive	Ads are **persuasive** messages to make people buy products.
impressive	im•pres•sive	Her train layout filled the entire room and was very **impressive**.
ritual	rit•u•al	Many Native American tribes held a harvest **ritual**.
factual	fac•tu•al	Not everything you see in print is **factual**.
mutual	mu•tu•al	They ended their partnership by **mutual** agreement.
eventually	e•ven•tu•al•ly	The weather will **eventually** get better.
actually	ac•tu•al•ly	He's **actually** quite tall for his age.

Copy the spelling words in the order they appear above. Number them in order from A–Z. You may need to look as far as the third letter. Then write the words in A–Z order.

Word	Number	A–Z Order
1.		
2.		
3.		
4.		
5.		
6.		
7.		
8.		
9.		
10.		
11.		
12.		
13.		
14.		
15.		

Word Endings: "sive" & "tual" (cont.)

Finding Synonyms

Look up each spelling word in a dictionary or a thesaurus (if available). Find its **synonym** (word that means almost the same thing). Then write each spelling word on the line next to its synonym(s). To help you choose the best word, most list multiple synonyms.

Synonyms	Spelling Word
1. dynamite, TNT	
2. lavish, splendid, grand	
3. finally, ultimately	
4. huge, enormous	
5. overwhelming, extreme	
6. rude, disgusting	
7. actual, absolute, genuine	
8. reasonable, cheap	
9. influential, convincing	
10. spontaneous	
11. rite, ceremony, service	
12. greedy, jealous	
13. expansive, broad	
14. truly, really	
15. shared, common, joint	

Word Ending: "ment"

The word ending "ment" often stands for "action of."

Word	Syllables	In Context
instruments	in•stru•ments	Our band includes string **instruments**.
experiment	ex•per•i•ment	The science class conducted an **experiment** with duck eggs.
statement	state•ment	Rick's **statement** was misquoted by the newspaper.
elements	el•e•ments	Copper, nickel, and gold are all **elements**.
movement	move•ment	The robotic figure's **movement** made it appear lifelike.
measurements	mea•sure•ments	Please tell me the window's **measurements**.
environment	en•vi•ron•ment	Ferns will only grow in a shady, moist **environment**.
equipment	e•quip•ment	You need a backhoe and heavy **equipment** to clear the land.
department	de•part•ment	A **department** store carries a wide variety of merchandise.
apartment	a•part•ment	I rented the **apartment** above the bookstore.
arrangement	ar•range•ment	The women made a beautiful floral **arrangement**.
replacement	re•place•ment	We will provide a **replacement** for the defective oven.
agreement	a•gree•ment	They just couldn't reach an **agreement**.
judgment	judg•ment	The court's **judgment** was an 8-day jail sentence.
argument	ar•gu•ment	I could hear the boys' **argument** all the way down the hall.

Circle the word that's spelled correctly. Copy it on the line.

1. movment   moviment   movement   _____

2. envirment   environment   envirement   _____

3. statement   statment   staitment   _____

4. elments   elements   eliments   _____

5. experment   experiment   expiriment   _____

6. aparment   appartment   apartment   _____

7. replacement   replacmment   repacement   _____

8. judjement   judgment   judjement   _____

9. aggreement   agrement   agreement   _____

10. instruments   instriments   instrumens   _____

11. arangement   arrangement   arrangment   _____

12. equiptment   equitment   equipment   _____

13. deparment   department   deppartment   _____

14. arguement   argrument   argument   _____

15. measurements   mesurements   measurments   _____

Word Ending: "ment" *(cont.)*

Syllable Cymbals

Write each spelling word on the cymbal that matches its number of syllables. Write the syllables within each word using different colors.

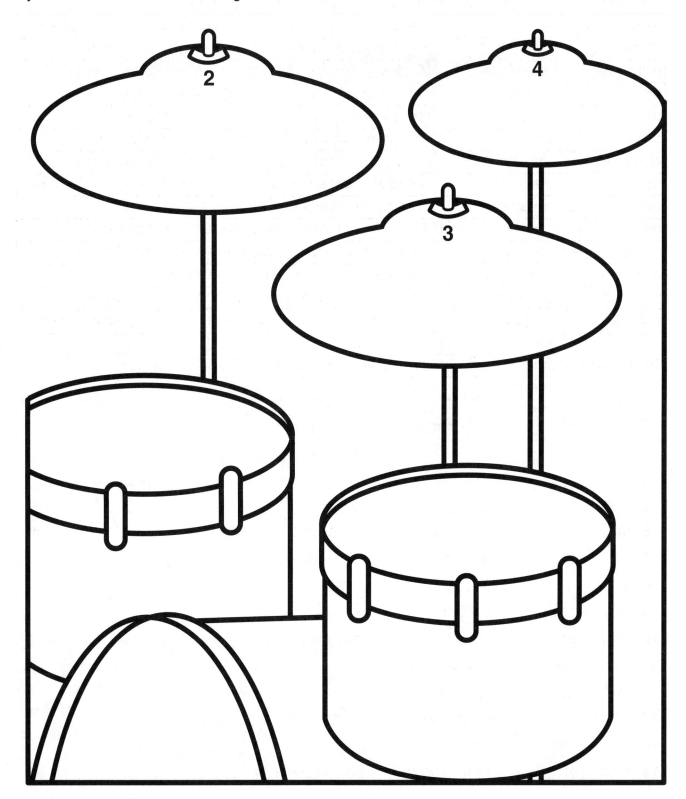

Word Endings: "sure," "cian," "cious," & "tious"

This group of word endings all sound as if they contain the letters "sh," yet none of them do. Just like the word "sure," the word ending "sure" is pronounced "shur." The word ending "cian" is pronounced "shun." This word ending always means a job title. The word endings "cious" and "tious" are pronounced "shus."

Word	Syllables	In Context
leisure	lei•sure	What do you like to do during your **leisure** time?
pressure	pres•sure	Apply **pressure** above the wound to slow down the bleeding.
treasure	trea•sure	The pirates hid their **treasure** on an island.
pleasure	plea•sure	It would be a **pleasure** to go with you to the concert.
reassure	re•as•sure	Let me **reassure** you that every precaution is being taken.
magician	ma•gi•cian	The **magician** performed nine amazing tricks.
musician	mu•si•cian	My dad is a **musician**; he plays the saxophone.
politician	pol•i•ti•cian	The **politician** shook hands with everyone in the room.
technician	tech•ni•cian	The computer **technician** finally figured out what was wrong.
precious	pre•cious	Diamonds, emeralds, and rubies are **precious** gems.
delicious	de•li•cious	A **delicious** aroma drifted out from the restaurant.
spacious	spa•cious	Her apartment isn't cramped at all; in fact, it's very **spacious**.
cautiously	cau•tious•ly	The woman **cautiously** drove through the fog.
infectious	in•fec•tious	Chickenpox is very **infectious**; almost everyone catches it.
repetitious	rep•e•ti•tious	This speech is boring because it's too **repetitious**.

Choose the best spelling word to complete each sentence. Use each word once.

1. We smelled the _____ aroma of chocolate chip cookies baking.

2. A senator is a _____; he or she must be elected to office.

3. Did he _____ you that your ferret will recover?

4. Your report is too _____. You mention the same dates over and over again.

5. Resist _____ from friends to use alcohol or tobacco.

6. During my _____ time, I play golf.

7. The child _____ peeked around the door.

8. The _____ needed new strings for her guitar.

9. The children got great _____ by riding every ride at least three times.

10. Her laughter was so _____ that soon we were all giggling, too.

11. Next the _____ pulled a dove out of a clear glass vase!

12. The _____ chest held gold and silver coins, pearls, and gems.

13. Since the office was so _____, we had plenty of room to spread out.

14. The _____ on duty repaired the computer.

15. That bracelet is very _____ to me because it belonged to my late grandmother.

Word Endings: "sure," "cian," "cious," & "tious" *(cont.)*

Word Scramble

Unscramble the words below to form spelling words from this lesson. Put the numbered letters on the lines below to find the answer to the riddle.

Example: etrax   l   u   s   c   i   o   u   s

1. nicechanti   ___ ___ ___ ___(1) ___ ___ ___ ___ ___ ___

2. croupsie   ___ ___ ___ ___ ___(2) ___ ___

3. irulese   ___ ___ ___(3) ___ ___ ___ ___

4. iscolduei   ___(4) ___ ___ ___ ___ ___ ___ ___ ___

5. superser   ___ ___ ___ ___ ___(5) ___ ___ ___

6. utisycuola   ___ ___ ___ ___ ___ ___ ___ ___(6) ___

7. uresater   ___(7) ___ ___ ___ ___ ___ ___

8. oupertsitie   ___ ___ ___ ___ ___ ___ ___ ___ ___ ___ ___

9. aruresse   ___ ___(8) ___ ___ ___ ___ ___

10. isamcinu   ___ ___ ___ ___ ___ ___ ___ ___

11. leasepur   ___ ___ ___ ___ ___ ___ ___ ___

12. copitlanii   ___ ___ ___ ___ ___ ___ ___ ___ ___(9) ___

13. coufinsite   ___ ___ ___ ___ ___ ___ ___ ___ ___ ___

14. gaincami   ___ ___ ___ ___(10) ___ ___ ___ ___

15. uscapsio   ___ ___(11) ___ ___ ___ ___ ___ ___

Riddle: Where can you always find money?

___ ___   ___ ___ ___   ___ ___ ___ ___ ___ ___ ___ ___ ___ ___
3   9   7   1   8   4   3   10   7   3   2   9   11   5   6

Word Ending: "sion"

The word ending "sion" is not pronounced the way it looks. It is pronounced "shun." There's no logical reason for this; it's just how it is!

Word	Syllables	In Context
division	di•vi•sion	Have you memorized your **division** facts yet?
television	tel•e•vi•sion	I watch less than three hours of **television** daily.
mansion	man•sion	She lives in that **mansion** on the hill overlooking town.
tension	ten•sion	There is often **tension** between nations in the Middle East.
admission	ad•mis•sion	Keith has guaranteed **admission** to a state college.
decision	de•ci•sion	It was hard to reach this **decision**.
occasionally	oc•ca•sion•al•ly	We do **occasionally** have red helmets in stock.
conclusion	con•clu•sion	This title is the **conclusion** of the six-book series.
discussion	dis•cus•sion	Our class had a lively **discussion** about the election.
dimensions	di•men•sions	Please tell me the **dimensions** of the room.
impression	im•pres•sion	Barry wants to make a good **impression** on Elaine.
possessions	pos•ses•sions	The Hortons lost all of their **possessions** in the fire.
professional	pro•fes•sion•al	The starting salary for this **professional** position is $75,000.
expression	ex•pres•sion	Abigail had a startled **expression** on her face.
expansion	ex•pan•sion	When will the school **expansion** project be completed?

Many words are formed from similar "roots." For example, the Greek root "ped" means "foot." You see this root in words such as *pedestrian*, *pedal*, *biped*, and *pedestal*. Write the spelling word that has a similar root to the word given.

1. conclude _____

2. manor (estate) _____

3. impressed _____

4. televised _____

5. expanding _____

6. divide _____

7. admit _____

8. occasion _____

9. possessive _____

10. professor _____

11. diminish _____

12. tense _____

13. decide _____

14. expressive _____

15. discuss _____

Word Ending: "sion" (cont.)

Using a Dictionary

Guide words are in bold print at the top of each dictionary page. You look at them to see if the word you want falls between them.

Write each spelling word. Look up each one in a dictionary. What are the two guide words at the top of the page? Write the guide words.

Spelling Word	Left-Side Guide Word	Right-Side Guide Word
Example: recession	received	reckon
1.		
2.		
3.		
4.		
5.		
6.		
7.		
8.		
9.		
10.		
11.		
12.		
13.		
14.		
15.		

Word Endings: "cial" & "tial"

The word endings "cial" and "tial" are both pronounced "shuhl."

Word	Syllables	In Context
especially	es•pe•cial•ly	The baby is **especially** fond of this stuffed bear.
official	of•fi•cial	The **official** score was 13–2.
social	so•cial	At 96, she still had an active **social** life, attending many parties.
crucial	cru•cial	While making pudding, it's **crucial** to keep the milk from boiling.
commercial	com•mer•cial	The television **commercial** showed new games.
financial	fi•nan•cial	Their **financial** advisor chose six stocks for them to invest in.
artificial	ar•ti•fi•cial	Houseplants often need **artificial** light.
beneficial	ben•e•fi•cial	Vitamin C is **beneficial** in preventing the common cold.
initial	in•i•tial	The **initial** report stated that three people were injured.
essential	es•sen•tial	It's **essential** to eat foods from all five food groups.
partial	par•tial	The police found only a **partial** fingerprint at the crime scene.
potential	po•ten•tial	You have the **potential** to be an honor student.
substantial	sub•stan•tial	A **substantial** amount of snow had fallen overnight.
confidential	con•fi•den•tial	This is **confidential** data; it must not be shared with anyone.
influential	in•flu•en•tial	The **influential** citizen convinced the mayor to vote "No."

Is the **boldfaced** word spelled wrong? If it is not correct, write it correctly in the middle column. If it is right, circle **OK**.

1. Your bank account number must be kept **confidential**.		OK
2. It's **crucial** to stop at a red traffic light.		OK
3. A pet bird may need a source of **artifical** light indoors.		OK
4. This ad will attract **potential** clients to your firm.		OK
5. I have only a **partial** map of the site.		OK
6. I'm not **especialy** fond of truffles.		OK
7. Dora's **initial** reaction was shock.		OK
8. Flour is an **essential** ingredient in cookies.		OK
9. His **oficial** title is Recreation and Parks Director.		OK
10. The tornado caused **sustantial** damage.		OK
11. He's a **finantial** investment counselor.		OK
12. Stuart enjoys **social** studies.		OK
13. It's **benficial** to take vitamins daily.		OK
14. That's not a very **influential** argument.		OK
15. The **comericial** announced a 25-percent-off sale.		OK

Word Endings: "cial" & "tial" *(cont.)*

Across

2. The jacket looks as if it's made of _____ leather.
5. Jacki has the _____ to be an opera soprano.
6. The _____ deer hunting season begins on November 15.
9. Please shred all _____ documents before disposing of them.
10. Is this area zoned for residential dwellings or _____ buildings?
11. Latasha was _____ fond of cherry cobbler.
12. Here's a _____ payment toward the total amount I owe you.
15. Martin inherited a _____ sum of money from his great uncle.

Down

1. Keeping all your vaccinations current is _____ to your health.
3. My older sister is getting some _____ aid toward her college tuition.
4. Preserving land is _____ in maintaining wild animal populations.
7. The fashions on TV are _____ to the styles many Americans wear.
8. With a computer, it's _____ to frequently save your work.
13. You must capitalize the _____ letter of the first word in every sentence.
14. He feels shy and awkward in _____ gatherings like parties.

Word Ending: "tion"

Word	Syllables	In Context
directions	di•rec•tions	Don gave me the **directions** to your house.
section	sec•tion	The teacher said to read just this **section** of the chapter.
action	ac•tion	Why don't you take some **action** to change things?
attention	at•ten•tion	Please pay **attention** to me.
mention	men•tion	Did Carla **mention** that she'd be late tonight?
collection	col•lec•tion	Joe is proud of his rare coin **collection**.
production	pro•duc•tion	The factory began **production** of its newest skateboard model.
selection	se•lec•tion	The store had a wide **selection** of colorful kites.
invention	in•ven•tion	Jayne's latest **invention** is sure to be a big success.
description	de•scrip•tion	The brochure's **description** made the resort sound wonderful.
protection	pro•tec•tion	A smoke detector provides **protection** for your family.
suggestion	sug•ges•tion	Sheila has a **suggestion** to make.
election	e•lec•tion	The **election** was so close, it took days to find out who won.
instructions	in•struc•tions	Check the game's **instructions** to see what to do in this case.
introduction	in•tro•duc•tion	The book's **introduction** made me want to read more.

Choose the best word from the list above to complete each sentence. Write it on the line. Use each word once. Skip those you can't figure out and return to them once you've done the others.

1. The _____ of the steam engine made automation possible.

2. Please turn your _____ to the display on your left.

3. Will you please write the _____ for the book?

4. Peter Ridowitz won the _____ for governor.

5. Your _____ is brilliant.

6. The dairy farm's milk _____ increased dramatically.

7. Don't worry; I won't _____ your mistake to anyone.

8. Which _____ of the museum did you find most interesting?

9. Can you give me _____ to the county fair?

10. William has a small baseball card _____.

11. I bought my little brother two _____ figures of his birthday.

12. Let's read the _____ to figure out how to put it together.

13. A helmet gives head _____ to bikers, skateboarders, and inline skaters.

14. Do the police have an eyewitness _____ of the suspect?

15. We have a good _____ of coffee tables in that price range.

Word Ending: "tion" *(cont.)*

Different Kinds of Sentences

Write spelling words 1–5 in exclamatory sentences. An exclamatory sentence communicates strong emotion or surprise.

Exclamatory Sentences End with an Exclamation Point

1. _____
2. _____
3. _____
4. _____
5. _____

Write spelling words 6–10 in **declarative** sentences. A declarative sentence makes a statement. **Example:** *We went to the store.*

Declarative Sentences End with a Period

6. _____
7. _____
8. _____
9. _____
10. _____

Write spelling words 11–15 in **interrogative** sentences. An interrogative sentence asks a question. **Example:** *Did you go to the store?*

Interrogative Sentences End with a Question Mark

11. _____
12. _____
13. _____
14. _____
15. _____

Word Ending: "ation"

An "a" just before "tion" is usually pronounced with as a long /a/.

Word	Syllables	In Context
information	in•for•ma•tion	Do you have any **information** on the store's hours?
station	sta•tion	Jill stood in the bus **station** and waved goodbye.
population	pop•u•la•tion	The **population** in our country is growing slowly.
operation	op•er•a•tion	Bianca needs an **operation** on her foot.
education	ed•u•ca•tion	Tim realizes that he'll benefit from a good **education**.
organization	or•ga•ni•za•tion	The rummage sale raised $1,650 for our **organization**.
observation	ob•ser•va•tion	After careful **observation**, I know these birds will eat toads.
location	lo•ca•tion	This would be a great **location** for a shopping mall.
investigation	in•ves•ti•ga•tion	The detective's **investigation** finally led to the criminal.
illustrations	il•lus•tra•tions	She does the **illustrations** for children's books.
punctuation	punc•tu•a•tion	Quinn needs to focus on improving his **punctuation**.
explanation	ex•pla•na•tion	What's your **explanation** for this mess?
situation	sit•u•a•tion	The flood caused an emergency **situation** in the town.
equation	e•qua•tion	This is a difficult **equation**; I don't know how to solve it.
pronunciation	pro•nun•ci•a•tion	What's the proper **pronunciation** of that word?

Copy the spelling words in the order they appear above. Number them in order from A–Z. You may need to look as far as the third letter. Then write the words in A–Z order.

Word	Number	A–Z Order
1.		
2.		
3.		
4.		
5.		
6.		
7.		
8.		
9.		
10.		
11.		
12.		
13.		
14.		
15.		

Word Ending: "ation" (cont.)

Phone Code

Telephones have numbers and letters on their keys. The spelling words are written below in phone code. Periods separate each digit (letter). Decode each spelling word and write it in the second column. It may help to decode on a piece of scrap paper.

Hint: Use the number of letters in each word to help you narrow down your choices. For example, just three of the spelling words have 9 letters.

1	2 ABC	3 DEF
4 GHI	5 JKL	6 MNO
7 PRS	8 TUV	9 WXY
*	0 QZ	#

Phone Code for Word	Spelling Word
Example: 2.6.6.4.7.2.8.8.5.2.8.4.6.6.7	congratulations
1. 6.7.4.2.6.4.0.2.8.4.6.6	
2. 5.6.2.2.8.4.6.6	
3. 6.7.3.7.2.8.4.6.6	
4. 3.0.8.2.8.4.6.6	
5. 4.6.8.3.7.8.4.4.2.8.4.6.6	
6. 7.8.6.2.8.8.2.8.4.6.6	
7. 4.5.5.8.7.8.7.2.8.4.6.6.7	
8. 3.3.8.2.2.8.4.6.6	
9. 7.6.7.8.5.2.8.4.6.6	
10. 7.4.8.8.2.8.4.6.6	
11. 7.7.6.6.8.6.2.4.2.8.4.6.6	
12. 4.6.3.6.7.6.2.8.4.6.6	
13. 3.9.7.5.2.6.2.8.4.6.6	
14. 6.2.7.3.7.8.2.8.4.6.6	
15. 7.8.2.8.4.6.6	

Word Endings: Vowels Before "tion"

An "i" just before "tion" is usually short. Other vowels (**a**, **o**, **u**) that come just before "tion" are long.

Word	Syllables	In Context
position	po•si•tion	I don't like the vase in that **position**; let's move it.
composition	com•po•si•tion	Grace's **composition** was the best in the class.
definition	def•i•ni•tion	The **definition** of daughter is "female offspring."
traditional	tra•di•tion•al	We had a **traditional** Thanksgiving feast.
vacation	va•ca•tion	My family went on **vacation** to Alaska.
imagination	i•mag•i•na•tion	Brian has a wonderful **imagination**—just look at his painting!
variation	var•i•a•tion	I don't see any **variation** in the pattern.
civilization	civ•i•li•za•tion	The ancient Greek **civilization** was very advanced.
association	as•so•ci•a•tion	The Friends of the Library **association** held a book sale.
vibration	vi•bra•tion	They could feel the train's **vibration** on the trestle.
emotions	e•mo•tions	Try to be thoughtful of others' **emotions**.
solution	so•lu•tion	What's your **solution** to this problem?
revolution	rev•o•lu•tion	The **revolution** caused great unrest in the country.
pollution	pol•lu•tion	Fortunately, water **pollution** is decreasing.
Constitution	Con•sti•tu•tion	The United States **Constitution** can only be altered by amendments.

Many words are formed from similar "roots." For example, the Greek root "phon" means "sound." You see this root in words such as *telephone*, *microphone*, *symphony*, and *phonics*.

Write the spelling word that has the same root as the word given.

1. vary _____

2. solve _____

3. vibrate _____

4. emotional _____

5. positive _____

6. revolt _____

7. definite _____

8. associate _____

9. compose _____

10. image _____

11. constituents _____

12. tradition _____

13. civilians _____

14. polluted _____

15. vacant _____

Word Endings: Vowels Before "tion" *(cont.)*

Using a Dictionary

Guide words are in bold print at the top of each dictionary page. You look at them to see if the word you want falls between them.

Write each spelling word. Look up each one in a dictionary. What are the two guide words at the top of the page? Write the guide words.

Spelling Word	Left-Side Guide Word	Right-Side Guide Word
Example: confirmation	conductor	confiscate
1.		
2.		
3.		
4.		
5.		
6.		
7.		
8.		
9.		
10.		
11.		
12.		
13.		
14.		
15.		

Assessment 1

Fill in the circle that has the underlined word spelled incorrectly. If all choices are correct, fill in "e."

1. ⓐ foreign country	ⓑ barely believable	
ⓒ very disappointed	ⓓ mischevous cat	ⓔ all correct
2. ⓐ favorite companion	ⓑ don't interrupt	
ⓒ sign languge	ⓓ became necessary	ⓔ all correct
3. ⓐ handsome millionaire	ⓑ ridiculous idea	
ⓒ acceptable procedure	ⓓ incredible accuracy	ⓔ all correct
4. ⓐ old equiptment	ⓑ possessive wife	
ⓒ leisure time	ⓓ general admission	ⓔ all correct
5. ⓐ essential supplies	ⓑ close attention	
ⓒ ancient civlization	ⓓ non-profit organization	ⓔ all correct
6. ⓐ earned privilege	ⓑ unkept room	
ⓒ dissatisfied client	ⓓ misspelled words	ⓔ all correct
7. ⓐ dangerous intersetion	ⓑ communicate often	
ⓒ large mortgage	ⓓ military action	ⓔ all correct
8. ⓐ Islamic religion	ⓑ hideous sight	
ⓒ not knowlegeable	ⓓ irresponsible decision	ⓔ all correct
9. ⓐ persuasive person	ⓑ faulty judgment	
ⓒ jazz musician	ⓓ happens occasionally	ⓔ all correct
10. ⓐ influential speech	ⓑ unclear description	
ⓒ wrong pronunciation	ⓓ seperate rooms	ⓔ all correct
11. ⓐ U.S. Constitution	ⓑ miscellanious stuff	
ⓒ unmistakable odor	ⓓ distinct personality	ⓔ all correct
12. ⓐ employees' committee	ⓑ still self-sufficient	
ⓒ great courage	ⓓ temporary lodgings	ⓔ all correct
13. ⓐ emphasize enough	ⓑ changeable weather	
ⓒ gorgous doll	ⓓ impossible deadline	ⓔ all correct
14. ⓐ eventualy won	ⓑ big argument	
ⓒ repetitious article	ⓓ long discussion	ⓔ all correct
15. ⓐ artificial flowers	ⓑ good selection	
ⓒ on-going investigation	ⓓ wheel's revolvution	ⓔ all correct
16. ⓐ familiar face	ⓑ Missisippi River	
ⓒ don't disrupt	ⓓ unusual markings	ⓔ all correct
17. ⓐ in self-defense	ⓑ best advantage	
ⓒ extraordinary bravery	ⓓ in comparison	ⓔ all correct
18. ⓐ might recognize	ⓑ outrageous idea	
ⓒ flexable tubing	ⓓ replaceable filter	ⓔ all correct
19. ⓐ delcious pie	ⓑ carpeting measurements	
ⓒ factual statement	ⓓ difficult time	ⓔ all correct
20. ⓐ volunteer association	ⓑ your suggestion	
ⓒ beneficial treatment	ⓓ real explaination	ⓔ all correct

Assessment 2

Darken the circle of the one word that is spelled incorrectly in each row.

1. (a) association   (b) explanation
   (c) suggestion   (d) decision   (e) benficial

2. (a) outragous   (b) delicious
   (c) measurements   (d) actually   (e) irresponsible

3. (a) replaceable   (b) recognize
   (c) contemporary   (d) self-defence   (e) advantage

4. (a) Missouri   (b) disrupt
   (c) unusual   (d) familiar   (e) comparision

5. (a) revolution   (b) selection
   (c) investgation   (d) artificial   (e) discussion

6. (a) repetitious   (b) eventually
   (c) impossible   (d) arguement   (e) changeable

7. (a) gorgeous   (b) self-suffcient
   (c) emphasize   (d) temporary   (e) encourage

8. (a) separate   (b) miscellaneous
   (c) commitee   (d) distinct   (e) unmistakable

9. (a) pronounciation   (b) pollution
   (c) description   (d) influential   (e) musician

10. (a) judgment   (b) occassionally
    (c) persuasive   (d) responsible   (e) hideous

11. (a) plausible   (b) religion
    (c) morgage   (d) military   (e) interpreter

12. (a) disatisfied   (b) communication
    (c) misspelled   (d) unkempt   (e) civilization

13. (a) organization   (b) attention
    (c) essential   (d) admission   (e) priviledge

14. (a) treasure   (b) equipment
    (c) incredible   (d) jealous   (e) possesive

15. (a) millionaire   (b) language
    (c) beverage   (d) aceptable   (e) international

16. (a) disappointed   (b) tecnician
    (c) foreign   (d) vacuum   (e) embarrass

17. (a) flammable   (b) necessary
    (c) accomodate   (d) disease   (e) unfortunately

18. (a) valuable   (b) infectious
    (c) situation   (d) extrordinary   (e) vegetables

19. (a) confidential   (b) replacment
    (c) misinterpret   (d) interior   (e) apologize

20. (a) licence   (b) excessive
    (c) elementary   (c) courteous   (e) illegible

Answer Key

Page 4
1. familiar
2. accommodate, appropriate
3. vacuum
4. license
5. separate
6. irrelevant
7. guarantee
8. calendar
9. foreign
10. embarrass
11. privilege
12. weird
13. rhythm
14. a lot

Page 5
1. license
2. guarantee
3. appropriate
4. calendar
5. vacuum
6. weird
7. irrelevant
8. rhythm
9. embarrass
10. a lot
11. accommodate
12. privilege
13. familiar
14. foreign
15. separate

Page 6
1. uncertain
2. unreliable
3. unexpected
4. unwelcome
5. unusual
6. unable
7. uncommon
8. untied
9. unreasonable
10. unfortunately
11. unmistakable
12. unhappy
13. uninjured
14. unknown
15. unkempt
16. neat

Page 7
1. uninjured
2. unwelcome
3. unkempt
4. unmistakable
5. unable
6. unusual
7. uncertain
8. unreliable
9. untied
10. unexpected
11. unhappy
12. uncommon
13. unfortunately
14. unknown
15. unreasonable

Riddle: chili today, hot tamale

Page 8
1. disapproved
2. disadvantage
3. dissolve
4. distinct
5. discuss
6. disease
7. dissatisfied
8. distribute
9. discouraged
10. disappointed
11. disrupt
12. discovery
13. disturb
14. disorganized
15. disaster

Page 9
Answers will vary.

Page 10
1. antonym
2. antonym
3. synonym
4. synonym
5. synonym
6. synonym
7. antonym
8. antonym
9. antonym
10. antonym
11. synonym
12. synonym
13. synonym
14. Mississippi & Missouri

Page 11
2 syllables: mistakes, misjudged, misspelled, misplaced

3 syllables: misery, mischievous, misgivings, Missouri, misbehaves, misleading

4 syllables: miserable, Mississippi, misinterpret

5 syllables: miscellaneous, misunderstanding

Page 12
1. company
2. complex
3. computer
4. compass, comments
5. companion, comparison, communication
6. combined, command, complicated
7. complete, compare, committee, communicate

Page 13

Page 14
1. interview
2. OK
3. OK
4. self-confidence
5. interesting
6. self-defense
7. OK
8. OK
9. intersection
10. interior
11. OK
12. interrupt
13. OK
14. self-sufficient
15. intervene

Page 15
Lower side of the scale has "inter" words; higher side of scale has "self" words.

Page 16
1. beverage
2. encourage
3. voyage
4. luggage
5. marriage
6. language
7. average
8. package
9. damage
10. carriage
11. message
12. courage
13. advantage
14. manager
15. mortgage

Answer Key *(cont.)*

Page 17

1. mortgage
2. carriage
3. luggage
4. message
5. courage
6. marriage
7. beverage
8. language
9. voyage
10. manager
11. damage
12. encourage
13. advantage
14. package
15. average

Riddle: at a crustacean bus station

Page 18

1. vary; 14; contemporary
2. dictionary; 2; dictionary
3. necessary; 8; elementary
4. library; 6; extraordinary
5. ordinary; 9; imaginary
6. extraordinary; 4; library
7. military; 7; military
8. vocabulary; 15; necessary
9. primary; 10; ordinary
10. elementary; 3; primary
11. temporary; 13; solitary
12. imaginary; 5; stationary
13. stationary; 12; temporary
14. solitary; 11; vary
15. contemporary; 1; vocabulary

Page 19

1. ordinary
2. elementary
3. dictionary
4. contemporary
5. library
6. primary
7. solitary
8. extraordinary
9. vary
10. imaginary
11. vocabulary
12. stationary
13. temporary
14. necessary
15. military

Page 20

1. opinion
2. fashion
3. region
4. religion
5. apologize
6. emphasize
7. billion
8. recognize
9. onions
10. organize
11. champion
12. pavilion
13. realize
14. millionaire
15. memorize

Page 21

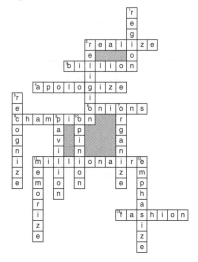

Page 22

1. gorgeous
2. nervous, numerous
3. jealous
4. ridiculous
5. famous, fabulous
6. outrageous
7. hideous
8. dangerous
9. marvelous
10. enormous
11. courageous, courteous, continuous

Page 23

1. antonym
2. synonym
3. synonym
4. antonym
5. synonym
6. synonym
7. antonym
8. synonym
9. antonym
10. antonym
11. antonym
12. antonym
13. antonym
14. synonym
15. synonym

Page 24

1. changeable
2. OK
3. comfortable
4. OK
5. replaceable
6. vulnerable
7. OK
8. OK
9. valuable
10. OK
11. OK
12. disposable
13. OK
14. knowledgeable
15. vegetables

Page 25

1. suitable
2. acceptable
3. comfortable
4. knowledgeable
5. replaceable
6. believable
7. vegetables
8. changeable
9. capable
10. vulnerable
11. valuable
12. disposable
13. remarkable
14. available
15. flammable

Riddle: like shaken bacon

Page 26

1. irresponsible
2. possible
3. edible
4. illegible
5. visible
6. flexible
7. impossible
8. invisible
9. terrible
10. sensible
11. audible
12. incredible
13. plausible
14. divisible
15. responsible

Page 27

Answers will vary.

Page 28

1. inexpensive; 9; actually
2. possessive; 14; eventually
3. excessive; 3; excessive
4. extensive; 5; explosives
5. explosives; 4; extensive
6. impulsive; 8; factual
7. massive; 10; impressive
8. offensive; 12; impulsive
9. persuasive; 13; inexpensive
10. impressive; 7; massive
11. ritual; 15; mutual
12. factual; 6; offensive
13. mutual; 11; persuasive
14. eventually; 2; possessive
15. actually; 1; ritual

Page 29

1. explosives
2. impressive
3. eventually
4. massive
5. excessive
6. offensive
7. factual
8. inexpensive
9. persuasive
10. impulsive
11. ritual

Answer Key (cont.)

12. possessive
13. extensive
14. actually
15. mutual

Page 30
1. movement
2. environment
3. statement
4. elements
5. experiment
6. apartment
7. replacement
8. judgment
9. agreement
10. instruments
11. arrangement
12. equipment
13. department
14. argument
15. measurements

Page 31
2 syllables: statement, movement, judgment

3 syllables: instruments, elements, measurements, equipment, department, apartment, arrangement, replacement, agreement, argument

4 syllables: experiment, environment

Page 32
1. delicious
2. politician
3. reassure
4. repetitious
5. pressure
6. leisure
7. cautiously
8. musician
9. pleasure
10. infectious
11. magician
12. treasure
13. spacious
14. technician
15. precious

Page 33
1. technician
2. precious
3. leisure
4. delicious
5. pressure
6. cautiously
7. treasure
8. repetitious
9. reassure
10. musician
11. pleasure
12. politician
13. infectious
14. magician
15. spacious

Riddle: in the dictionary

Page 34
1. conclusion
2. mansion
3. impression
4. television
5. expansion
6. division
7. admission
8. occasionally
9. possession
10. professional
11. dimension
12. tension
13. decision
14. expression
15. discussion

Page 35
Answers will vary based on dictionary used.

Page 36
1. OK
2. OK
3. artificial
4. OK
5. OK
6. especially
7. OK
8. OK
9. official
10. substantial
11. financial
12. OK
13. beneficial
14. OK
15. commercial

Page 37

Page 38
1. invention
2. attention
3. introduction
4. election
5. suggestion
6. production
7. mention
8. section
9. directions
10. collection
11. action
12. instructions
13. protection
14. description
15. selection

Page 39
Answers will vary.

Page 40
1. information; 5; education
2. station; 15; equation
3. population; 11; explanation
4. operation; 9; illustrations
5. education; 1; information
6. organization; 10; investigation
7. observation; 8; location
8. location; 7; observation
9. investigation; 6; operation
10. illustrations; 4; organization
11. punctuation; 13; population
12. explanation; 3; pronunciation
13. situation; 14; punctuation
14. equation; 2; situation
15. pronunciation; 12; station

Page 41
1. organization
2. location
3. operation
4. equation
5. investigation
6. punctuation
7. illustrations
8. education
9. population
10. situation
11. pronunciation
12. information
13. explanation
14. observation
15. station

Page 42
1. variation
2. solution
3. vibration
4. emotions
5. position
6. revolution
7. definition
8. association
9. composition
10. imagination
11. Constitution
12. traditional
13. civilization
14. pollution
15. vacation

Page 43
Answers will vary based on dictionary used.

Page 44
1. d	6. b	11. b	16. b
2. c	7. a	12. e	17. e
3. e	8. c	13. c	18. c
4. a	9. e	14. a	19. a
5. c	10. d	15. d	20. d

Page 45
1. e	6. d	11. c	16. b
2. a	7. b	12. a	17. c
3. d	8. c	13. e	18. d
4. e	9. a	14. e	19. b
5. c	10. b	15. d	20. a